EXPLORING THE UNKNOWN

OUT-OF-BODY EXPERIENCES

Carl R. Green
and
William R. Sanford

Illustrated by Keith Robinson

ENSLOW PUBLISHERS, INC.

Bloy St. & Ramsey Ave.   P.O. Box 38
Box 777   Aldershot
Hillside, N.J. 07205   Hants GU12 6BP
U.S.A.   U.K.

Library of Congress Cataloging-in-Publication Data

Green, Carl R.
    Out-of-body experiences/Carl R. Green and William R. Sanford ;
illustrated by Keith Robinson.
        p. cm. — (Exploring the unknown)
    Includes bibliographical references and index.
    Summary: Examines two similar phenomena, near-death and out-of-
body experiences, in which people are separated from their bodies
and reports cases of people who claim to have such experiences.
    ISBN 0-89490-457-4
    1. Astral projection—Juvenile literature. 2. Near-death
experiences—Juvenile literature. 3. Astral projection—Case
studies—Juvenile literature. 4. Near-death experiences—Case
studies—Juvenile literature. [1. Astral projection. 2. Near-
death experiences.] I. Sanford, William R. (William Reynolds),
1927–   . II. Title. III. Series.
BF1389.A7G72 1993
133.9—dc20   93-9172
                                                      CIP
                                                      AC

Printed in the United States of America

10 9 8 7 6 5 4 3 2 1

Photo Credits: Courtesy of Denver Public Library, Western History Depart-
ment, p. 28; Carl R. Green & William R. Sanford, pp. 37, 39, 40; Courtesy of
Dr. Elmar R. Gruber, Fortean Picture Library, p. 32; Courtesy of the National
Archives, pp. 15, 19, 22.

Illustrations Credit: Keith Robinson, pp. 8, 13, 21, 25, 27, 34, 36, 41.

Cover Photo: © Gary Bartholomew/West Light.

Contents

Authors' Note

Thanks to science, many of nature's great mysteries have been solved. Do you want to know about earthquakes or earthworms? There's probably an expert somewhere who can answer most of your questions. But wouldn't this be a boring world if we knew all there is to know? Perhaps that's why people want to believe that the mind does possess mysterious powers.

In this series you'll learn about these mysteries of the unknown:

- ✦ Fortune Telling
- ✦ Mysterious Mind Powers
- ✦ The Mystery of Dreams
- ✦ Out-of-Body Experiences
- ✦ Recalling Past Lives
- ✦ Seeing the Unseen

Do these truly exist? Some people say yes, others say no. Once you hear the debate, you can decide for yourself. While you're doing so, keep one thought in mind. In this field it is often hard to separate the real from the fake. It pays to be skeptical when setting out to explore the mysteries of the unknown.

1
A STRANGER IN THE CAPTAIN'S CABIN

IN 1828 first mate Robert Bruce's ship was six weeks out of Liverpool, sailing westward. He thought he knew everyone on board. So who—or what—was this apparition in the captain's cabin? The strange man was calmly writing on a slate. Shaken by the sight, Bruce hurried to tell the captain.

The captain rushed to his cabin. He found the slate, but the stranger was gone. Chalked on it were four words: *Steer to the Nor'west*.

Bruce swore he had not written the message. To prove it, he wrote the same words. His handwriting did not match. The puzzled captain tested his crew with the same results. Was there a stowaway on board? A search of the ship proved fruitless.

The captain studied the message. With the wind at his back, a course change would cost him little. He gave the order to steer to the northwest. Three hours later a lookout spotted a ship wrecked on an iceberg. Quickly, the ship's boats rescued the stranded crew. Bruce was watching as the survivors climbed aboard. One man caught his eye. He felt sure it was the stranger he had seen in the captain's cabin!

At the captain's request, the man wrote *Steer to the Nor'west* on the slate. His mouth fell open when the captain turned the slate over. The writing on both sides looked the same.

"I only wrote one of these," the man said. "Who wrote the other?"

The tale the man told was simple enough. He had fallen asleep on his stranded ship a few hours earlier. When he woke, he told his shipmates that help was on its way. He even described the rescue ship in exact detail.[1]

This story relates to an age-old mystery—the out-of-body experience, or OBE. The shipwrecked man seemingly left his body and traveled to the nearest ship. There his body double had chalked a message that led to his rescue. Why didn't he speak

★ ☾ ★ ☾ ★ ☾ ★ ☾ ★ ☾ ★ ☾ ★ ☾ ★ ☾ ★ ☾ ★ ☾ ★

USEFUL DEFINITIONS

Researchers who study the mind have worked hard to define the terms used to discuss out-of-body experiences. Here are a few of the key words:

astral travel—An older name for an OBE, still favored by psychics. During astral travel the "astral body" is said to journey outside the physical body. Some psychics claim they can go astral traveling any time they wish.

aura—An ever-changing energy field that psychics say surrounds a living plant, animal, or person. Psychics claim they can diagnose illness by the shape and color of a person's aura.

body double—The spirit body that leaves the real body during an OBE. Body doubles are also called astral bodies or doppelgängers.

extrasensory perception (ESP)—The ability to send or receive data without using the normal senses. ESP powers include clairvoyance, telepathy, and precognition.

near-death experience (NDE)—The feeling of having died and left one's body, only to return to take up one's life again.

out-of-body experience (OBE)—The feeling of leaving one's body to travel near and far. During OBEs people claim to travel as invisible energy bodies or as body doubles. These body doubles pass freely through walls and fly through space.

to Bruce? No one knows. OBEs do not obey the rules that govern daily life.

Near-death experiences (NDEs) are close cousins of the OBE. In a typical NDE, the Reverend J. L. Bertrand died . . . and then returned to life. Bertrand's NDE took place back in the 1800s while he was climbing in the Swiss Alps. Feeling weary, he told the guide to take the others in his group on to the top. As he lay in the snow, he found he could no longer move his arms and legs. His head ached with the cold. A thought popped into his mind: *I am freezing to death!*

All at once Bertrand felt himself leave his body. Looking down, he saw himself lying in the snow. He felt as though he was floating, held to that distant body by a thin cord. Soon he was high enough to see his fellow climbers. As he watched, the guide sneaked a chicken leg from the lunch pack. Bertrand felt sad that the cord still tied him to his old life.

Moments later he saw the returning climbers find his body. The guide rubbed the pale face and arms, trying to start blood flowing again. Bertrand felt himself being pulled downward. With a silent

Reverend Bertrand looks down on his rescuers during a near-death experience. Instead of feeling afraid, Bertrand felt regret that he was still tied to his earthbound body.

scream he passed back into his body. In that instant he knew he was alive once more. He sat up and scolded the startled guide for stealing the chicken leg.[2]

History is full of stories of OBEs and NDEs. Perhaps one day we will solve the puzzle of what they mean and how they happen. For now, we can only say that the mind hides its secrets all too well.

2
OBEs PAST AND PRESENT

OLGA WORRALL, alone and afraid, went to sleep with her bedroom light on. An hour later the British housewife awoke to see her husband standing by her bed. Although she knew he was away on a trip, she did not feel frightened.

"Put out the lights!" he seemed to say. Olga did as she was told. Then she went back to sleep.

When Worrall returned a few days later, he described what he thought was a dream. In the dream, he said, he walked through the house. As he neared the bedroom he saw that the light was on. Reaching out to switch it off, his hand went through the wall. That was when he told Olga to turn the light out. As soon as she obeyed, Worrall woke up—in his hotel bed.[1]

Were husband and wife sharing the same dream? After all, dreams take up two or more hours of each night's sleep. But research shows that dreams grow out of your own store of memories. No one else shares your dreams. Scientists who study reports of OBEs can only shake their heads. No hard evidence of the existence of astral bodies has been found. What people call OBEs, they say, may result from dream activity or an ESP event.

Whatever their origin, OBEs are far from dreamlike. Those who claim to have had an OBE

In some tribal cultures, priests and healers claim the power to travel out-of-body. They often return from these astral travels with advice and prophecies from the gods.

return with vivid reports of their travels. In a typical OBE, a body double leaves the sleeping body and floats above it. The body on the bed seems to shudder and become stiff. The double appears to be attached to the body, often by a silver cord. The astral body feels weightless and more alive than ever. The senses seem sharper, colors seem brighter.

Free to travel, the astral body walks through walls or soars high into the sky. During these journeys the cord stretches, but does not break. OBEs end when the body double returns to the physical body. Often it slips back without effort. At other times it enters with a jerk that wakes the sleeper. Either way, people who return from OBEs feel a sense of inner peace. Thoughts of death no longer fill them with fear.

No one knows when the first OBE took place. In early cultures priests often put themselves into trances. The trance, they said, allowed their souls to find and speak to the gods. In ancient Egypt, OBEs were part of religious beliefs. Each person was said to possess a *ka* and a *ba*. The *ka* was a body double that lived on in the tomb after death. That freed the *ba* to travel on to the next world. In modern India yogis enter trance states in which they claim to leave their bodies.

Over 2,500 years ago, the king of Syria led an army into Israel. Each time the Syrians attacked the Israelite army was waiting. "Who is giving away our plans?" the king roared. A member of the court told him about a prophet named Elisha. This Israelite, the man said, knows everything that is said in your tent. Perhaps the king believed that Elisha was using his astral body to visit his tent. Certain that he had found the spy, he laid siege to the prophet's city.

The Biblical prophet Elisha listens in as Syrian invaders plan an attack on the Israelites. Whether Elisha truly traveled out-of-body or not, the Syrians seemed to believe he did. The king set aside his battle plans and laid siege to Elisha's city.

Once again the king of Syria ran into powers far beyond his own. Elisha asked God to blind his foes. Then Elisha led the army of blind men into the Israelite camp. When their sight was restored the Syrians saw they were captives. They laid down their arms and marched home. [2]

Even the great thinkers of ancient times believed in OBEs. Plato was certain that the soul could leave the body and travel freely. Plotinus wrote of "being lifted out of the body into myself." [3]

The writer Hermotimus often wandered far from his stiff, still body. "Do not touch me while I am gone," he told his wife. But the wife, upset by her husband's absences, wanted to teach him a lesson. During one of his OBEs she asked two friends to move his body. Sadly, the two men turned out to be rivals, not friends. They declared that Herotimus was dead. Then they burned the body. [4]

When people study OBEs, some basic facts emerge.

✦ The world has changed but accounts of OBEs stay constant. An OBE described by a Texas cowboy closely resembles those reported by ancient Greeks.

★ ☾ ★ ☾ ★ ☾ ★ ☾ ★ ☾ ★ ☾ ★ ☾ ★ ☾ ★

LUCKY LINDY'S OBE

After World War I, brave pilots competed to set records for speed and distance. In 1927 Charles Lindbergh joined the ranks of aviation's great heroes. "Lucky Lindy" captured the nation's heart by flying nonstop from New York to Paris.

Once he was airborne, Lindbergh faced a flight of more than thirty hours. Twenty-two hours after takeoff the *Spirit of St. Louis* flew into a thick fog. As the plane droned on through the gray mist, Lindbergh fought to stay awake. Then, he revealed years later, he seemed to slip into an OBE.

Lindbergh wrote that he seemed to exist outside of "time and matter." He felt himself "departing from my body as I imagine a spirit would depart." Drifting upward and outward, he seemed to pass through the frame of the plane. Then he floated in midair, "far distant from the human form I left [behind]." All this time, he was bound to his body by a long cord. The cord was so thin, he wrote, "it could have been snapped by a breath."

Lindbergh knew that his "vision" could have been caused by fatigue. That kind of logic made sense—but the pilot set logic aside. He knew what he had seen and felt. The longer he lived, he wrote in his autobiography, the more he doubted that science has all the answers.[5]

Charles Lindbergh pioneered trans-Atlantic flights in his tiny plane, the Spirit of St. Louis. *During his 1927 flight he flew into a fog-bank and into an OBE. Because the experience was so personal, Lindbergh did not write about it until years later.*

Artist Edmund Sullivan's image of the rose-decked skeleton reminds viewers that death is never far away. People who return from OBEs and NDEs say they are relieved of this fear. Astral travel, they claim, proves there is life after death.

◆ Most people report only one OBE in a lifetime. Their OBEs often take place during stressful events such as an illness or car crash.

◆ No one who has had an OBE ever forgets it. People see their OBEs as proof that they will live on after death.

◆ OBEs are nearly always pleasant. But once the astral travel ends, most people refuse to talk about their journeys. They worry that their friends will think they have lost their minds.

◆ During on OBE people often "see" events they could not have seen with their normal senses. Experts suggest that the subjects may have used ESP—or they may have been astral traveling.

Scientific studies of OBEs face two problems. First, most people cannot summon an OBE at will. That fact makes it hard to set up controlled studies in a lab. Second, few astral travelers are trained observers. Most are too involved in their once-in-a-lifetime "trip" to make good mental notes.

3
TIED BY A SILVER CORD

IN ANCIENT EGYPT the *ba*, or body double, appeared as a bird with a human face. In later cultures the body double took on a clearly human form. The English writer D. H. Lawrence claimed to see his body double as he lay dying. The double, he said, had emerged from his physical body. As it stood in the corner of the room, it stared back at him.[1]

Astral travelers report that their body doubles cannot pick up a glass or open a book. But doors and walls cannot stop them. They fly to distant places by willing themselves to go there. Living people may see or sense their ghost-like presence. A few astral travelers find they can mind-speak to their friends and loved ones.

Writers seem to run into more OBEs than most people. Some famous names appear on the list: Edgar Allen Poe, Jack London, Emily Brontë, Mark Twain, Leo Tolstoy. In the late 1800s, Tolstoy was waiting at a train station in St. Petersburg, Russia, to greet D. D. Home, a famous psychic. He saw his friend step off the train—but then Home walked away. Annoyed at the snub, Tolstoy and his wife left the station. Three hours later the real Home stepped off his train and found the platform empty. When the men compared notes, both were amazed. Tolstoy became convinced that he had seen Home's body double.[2]

An American writer went through his own NDE in Italy during World War I. At the time, Ernest Hemingway was an ambulance driver. He was handing out candy to some soldiers on the day a shell burst nearby. Shrapnel tore into his legs. "I felt my soul . . . was coming right out of my body," Hemingway said. It was "like you'd pull a silk handkerchief out of a pocket by one corner. . . . It flew around and then came back and went in again and I wasn't dead anymore." In *A Farewell to Arms,* Hemingway puts his hero through a similar NDE.[3]

Author Ernest Hemingway was hit by shrapnel during World War I. He felt, he wrote, that his soul came out of his body "like you'd pull a silk handkerchief out of a pocket . . ."

A British author, William Gerhardie, claimed he could induce astral travel at will. Some of his journeys appear in his 1934 novel, *Resurrection*. Gerhardie writes that in one OBE he was pushed forward and placed on his feet. He staggered to the bedroom door, but could not turn the handle. His hand, he found, could not grip the knob. Looking back, he saw he was tied to his sleeping body by a glowing silver cord. When he floated through the front door, he felt he could fly anywhere he wished. But would his lifeline break? The question sent him flying back to his sleeping form, but all was well. Happy with his new freedom, he flew off again. The cord stretched to a frail thread but held firm. In the next instant his eyes snapped open. Gerhardie was back in bed, but he was certain his OBE had not been a dream.[4]

Gerhardie was not the first to describe a "silver cord" linking astral and physical bodies. The term appears in the Bible. The twelfth chapter of Ecclesiastes says, ". . . the mourners go about the streets before the silver cord is loosed." An American expert, Sylvan Muldoon, has tried to describe the cord. He believes it is one and one-half inches thick at the moment the astral and human bodies divide. As the astral body roams, the cord stretches as thin as a thread. Energy appears to pass through the cord from the astral body to the human body. Some writers report that it is attached to the forehead. Others say it is hooked to the body's navel or the back of the head. [5]

Those who glimpse astral travelers do not always see the silver cord. Mark Twain, the author of *Tom Sawyer,* wrote about such an event. Twain happened to see a stranger approach his house one

Author William Gerhardie claimed he could embark on an OBE whenever he wished. A glowing silver cord, he said, tied his astral body to his physical body. Almost everyone who returns from an OBE describes being tethered by such a cord.

Humorist Mark Twain was delighted when he saw what seemed to be a ghost. The apparition, he said, walked close to him—and then vanished. Twain was doubly surprised when he went into his house and saw the man waiting for him. OBE experts say his first contact must have been with the man's body double.

day. As he watched, the man walked to within twenty feet of where he stood. Then, in the blink of an eye, he was gone! Twain, a big fan of psychic events, was delighted. "I had seen a [ghost] at last, with my own eyes," he told himself. But more surprises lay ahead. When Twain entered the house, the stranger was waiting for him. A servant had welcomed the man into the house some time earlier.[6]

OBE experts believe that Twain saw the man's double, not a ghost. The man was already seated inside when his double retraced his steps to the door. Why would a body double repeat such a simple act? No one knows.

Strange as it seems, many people say they have had an OBE. In 1890, a British survey asked 17,000 people if they had been in touch with an astral body. Ten percent answered yes. Of these, one in three claimed to have seen doubles of living people. Almost a century later, a new survey turned up similar numbers. The 1975 study asked a thousand Americans if they had traveled out-of-body. Fourteen percent of the adults and 25 percent of the students said yes.[7] It appears that OBEs and NDEs are still going strong.

ASTRAL FLYER OR ASTRAL FRAUD?

Madame Helena Petrovna Blavatsky left Russia for the West in the 1800s. At first she wandered through Europe, holding séances. Her journeys then led her to New York, where she met Henry Olcott.

In 1875 Blavatsky and Olcott founded a group devoted to the study of what they called theosophy. They took the name for their beliefs from the Greek words for "god" and "wisdom." Followers gathered to learn "the magic of the ancients" from HPB (Helena Blavatsky's initials). Humans, she said, exist on many planes beyond the earthly one. HPB added that she often traveled via her astral body.

Critics attacked her work and revealed past scandals. To escape, HPB moved to India. There, she told the world, she made contact with a race of Masters. Theosophy revived and prospered.

The Society for Psychical Research (SPR) sent Richard Hodgson to check up on her. Hodgson soon decided that the "miracles" were just clever tricks. Although his report charged that HPB was a fraud, her followers ignored it. Their faith was rewarded a hundred years later. In 1986 the SPR agreed that Hodgson had not fully proven his case.[8]

4

STANDING AT THE EDGE

PRIVATE GEORGE RITCHIE came down with the flu during World War II. In the army hospital his fever peaked at 106.5 degrees. That night, as in a dream, he awoke and jumped out of bed. Behind him, he said later, he saw what looked like a dead man wearing his ring. Out in the hall, a nurse walked right through him. In the next instant he was flying through the night. When he tried to touch a phone line, his hand could not grasp it. Confused by his ghost-like state, he flew back to the hospital.

George flitted from room to room, looking at each sleeping man. At last he found his own body, covered by a sheet. All at once the room seemed to fill with light. George saw scenes from his life flash by. Then he saw wonderful new worlds beyond earth. "Look at all I have missed," George told himself. Then he slipped back inside his own body.

Seeing signs of life in the "corpse," a doctor injected George with a strong drug. In what the doctor called "a miracle," life surged back. Although George had been "dead" for nine minutes, his brain was not harmed. After the war his NDE led him to the task of caring for mental patients. He returned from the dead, he said, to

These four panels describe Private George Ritchie's NDE. One night George rose from his hospital bed, leaving what looked like a dead man behind. Out in the hall, he was surprised when a nurse walked right through him. After flying free through the night sky he returned to his body. There he saw a bright, supernatural light that filled him with hope for the future.

"learn about man and then serve God." He assured patients with similar tales that they were not insane.[1]

George Ritchie would enjoy a painting that hangs in Venice, Italy. Hieronymus Bosch painted "The Ascent of the Blessed" five centuries ago. The work shows the souls of the dead moving upward through a long tunnel. The tunnel leads to a pure yellow light and a divine being. People who have NDEs believe that death frees the soul to travel toward that healing light.

Kimberly Clark Sharp of Kansas knows about the light. When she was 22, she collapsed on a sidewalk. At first, she said, she found herself lost in a dense, gray fog. Then the fog vanished as the world flooded with light. "It was so bright, the sun is not as bright, yet it didn't hurt my eyes," she remembers. "It filled up everything, and I . . . was back with my Creator." Kimberly felt a sense of love beyond anything she had ever known. "It was heaven, more than ecstasy," she says. "It was a reunion of the highest order."[2]

Most accounts of NDEs repeat these feelings. People are aware of leaving their bodies, often by

Many people who report OBEs and NDEs tell similar stories. Their trips often begin in a long, dark tunnel. At the far end they encounter a brilliant light and a feeling of welcoming love. Within the light waits a divine being who counsels and teaches them.

floating outward. They can hear loved ones crying over their death. Instead of being frightened or in pain, they feel at peace. Many say they hear beautiful music. Long-dead friends appear to assure them that all is well. The world beyond this one, the astral travelers say, is hard to picture. The living cannot imagine a world without limits of time and space.

Many astral travelers say they fly at high speed through a tunnel, cave, or deep well. One said it was like "I was moving very, very fast in time and space. I was traveling through a tunnel. It didn't look like

This 1925 "spirit photograph" is an attempt to portray an OBE. During her astral travels Mrs. Martin (center) claimed to have met (left to right above her) her sister, her first husband, her child, and her brother-in-law. All were dead at the time the picture was said to be taken. Researchers later proved the photograph a fake.

a tunnel, but when you're in a tunnel, all you see is blackness around you."[3]

A light appears far ahead of the travelers. As the light grows brighter they see that it comes from a warm, loving being. Many think of the being as God. A wise voice counsels and teaches them. Sometimes they are allowed to view their lives from birth onward. This life review flashes past like a film run at high speed.

Then the NDE reaches a turning point. Death lies on the far side of a fence, a river, or beyond a line of trees. If you cross over, the voice says, you cannot come back. Many say they yearn for the peace that awaits "over there." They choose life, they say, because they still have work to do. Making that choice returns them to their bodies.

Many who have NDEs wonder if the experience was real. Hoping they are sane, they seek out others who have taken the same journey. Accepting the truth of their NDEs changes their lives. Given a new start, they pack each day with joy and good works. Because they no longer fear death, they live life to the fullest. People who never felt religious gain a strong new faith.[4]

NDEs LEAD TO A BETTER LIFE

Young Stuart Twemlow fell into a washtub. As he floated face down he felt relaxed and at peace. His life flashed before him. Instead of gratitude, he felt angry when his mother pulled him out. "I was enjoying where I was," he says. That NDE taught him to treasure each minute. "The NDE has a healing effect," he tells all who will listen.[5]

A young woman confirms Stuart's story. Pat (not her real name) recalls that her life was a mess. She was hooked on drugs and alcohol. Her NDE came during a suicide attempt. The brush with death, she says, taught her that "I'm supposed to be alive."

Pat gave up drugs and turned to helping other addicts. Before the NDE, she adds, "I was into blaming a lot of people. So it's almost like my whole . . . life has changed. . . . I'm reaching out a lot more than I did. I was really self-centered, and I'm growing out of that."[6]

Millions of Americans say they have had an NDE. Few of them, most likely, went looking for their close brush with death. Almost all of them agree on one thing. NDEs changed their lives—for the better.

Do NDEs give us a true picture of what happens when we die? No one knows for sure. After all, we have only the words of those who have escaped almost certain death. For its part, science rejects events that cannot be tested in a laboratory. For now, all we can do is wonder, hoping to learn more.

5
SCIENCE TAKES
A LOOK

ROBERT MONROE is one of the pioneers in OBE exploration. He reports that he first traveled out-of-body in 1958. Since then, Monroe claims to have had thousands of OBEs. Unlike many, he does not claim that astral journeys prove there is life after death. Take them for what they are, he says.

Monroe says most of his trips were pleasant, a few less so. At times he met other astral travelers. Some helped him, others attacked him. The attackers, he says, were evil, sub-human beings. As often happens in NDEs, he also met an "energy presence" of great power. Once in a while he found it hard to reenter his body. One scary moment came, he writes, when he slipped into a dead body by mistake.

To help his search, Monroe set up a lab to study

Is this a photo of an OBE, or only a bit of trick photography? Researchers at the Institut für Grenzgebiete der Psychologie in Germany produced this photo in 1982. The subject, shielded from distractions by colored goggles and headphones, was certainly trying to travel out-of-body.

OBEs in a scientific way. In 1975 he took out a patent on a device he calls Hemi-Sync. It is supposed to allow the mind to stay alert while the body falls asleep. In this state some subjects say they can leave their bodies. Like Monroe, they report contact with the spirits of the dead. Some add that they reach a state of bliss after meeting with a presence they believe is God.[1]

Science sets high standards in its search for truth. Monroe may be sincere, scientists say, but his work is flawed. Can he be trusted to run tests that might deny his beliefs? The data Monroe gathers is also suspect. Can his subjects be trusted? In their hypnotic state, they may be telling Monroe what they know he wants to hear.

Even if these doubts were resolved, questions would remain. Drug users, the mentally ill, and the sick sometimes "see" and "hear" weird sights and sounds. Some drug users, for instance, say they are floating in another world. Most mental hospitals have at least one inmate who "talks" to God. Patients coming out of surgery often hear voices no one else can hear. What about the bright light seen during an NDE? The firing of certain brain cells can create a point of light behind closed eyes. Seeing this light can give the illusion of being in a tunnel.

Back in 1966 Dr. Charles Tart of the University of Virginia tried to answer these doubts. His subject, known as Miss Z, said her OBEs had begun when she was a child. As part of the test, Tart placed a five-digit number on a high shelf. At one point during the fourth night the sleeping woman's brain waves showed a new pattern. Was this an OBE? When she woke up, Miss Z called off the correct numbers: 2-5-1-3-2. She had beaten odds of 99,999 to 1! Even then, Tart had to admit that the test did not provide final proof. Instead of an OBE, Miss Z might have used ESP to "see" the numbers.[2]

Dr. Charles Tart tried to apply scientific methods to the study of OBEs. In this test, he placed a five-digit number on a shelf high above his subject. On the fourth night, Miss Z claimed she had seen the numbers while traveling out-of-body. Against all odds, she named the numbers correctly.

Interest in OBEs kept growing. Dr. Robert Morris of the Psychical Research Foundation in North Carolina tried a new approach. He chose college student Keith Harary as his subject. In one test, Morris put Keith in a closed room. His task was to travel via OBE to a second building. There he would try to view cutout letters arranged by a technician. After each OBE, he was told to write down what he had seen. At times Keith beat the odds by scoring a high number of "hits." On other tries he scored poorly. Once he "saw" two people in the room. Morris checked and found that a second man had walked in during the test.[3]

Would cats be aware of an astral body? Keith began the new set of tests by making friends with a kitten named Spirit. Then the kitten was taken to a second room. An observer counted its every move. Researchers ran the test four times, but told Keith to contact the kitten only twice. Each time he did so, Spirit froze in his tracks. His eyes appeared to focus on something the observer could not see. During one non-OBE period Spirit meowed 37 times. When Keith was "present" during an OBE trial, the kitten did not meow at all.[4]

Keith Harary tested his ability to travel out-of-body with a cat named Spirit. An observer reported that during Keith's OBEs the cat froze in its tracks. Although the observer could not see anything, Spirit apparently sensed his friend's presence.

Do OBEs and NDEs exist? Despite all of the tests and first-hand reports, science is still skeptical. No one is giving up, however. Maybe the day will come when someone will explain the how and why of OBEs. If you wish, you can join in an OBE test. The American Society for Psychical Research in New York City has set up a special room. Anyone who has OBEs is urged to "visit" that room. If you do so, write to the ASPR and tell the researchers what you saw there. Send your letters to ASPR, 5 West 73rd St., New York, NY 10023.

A FILM STAR ENTERS A NEW AGE

Actress Shirley MacLaine is one of the millions who say they have traveled out-of-body. Unlike most of the others, she talks freely about her astral voyages.

Shirley had her first OBE while she was in Peru in 1975. One night, sitting in a warm bath, she began to stare at a candle flame. All at once she felt a tunnel open in her mind. "I felt myself become the flame," she writes. "I had no arms, no legs, no body. . . . I felt myself . . . rising out of my body until I began to soar."

Shirley's astral body flew into space. Below her lay the Andes Mountains. A shining silver cord linked her to her body. As she flew higher she found she could see the curve of the earth. At that point, she turned back. Gently she flowed back into her body. She felt, she says, like a bit of "Universal Energy."[5]

Thanks to her books and films, Shirley has become a leader in the New Age movement. New Agers believe in such things as OBEs, past lives, and the power of crystals. Mental health experts look at these beliefs and hold up a caution sign. Do not, they warn, let New Age psychics make your life choices for you.

New Age book stores have sprung up across the United States. Most stores sell crystals, charms, candles, and clothing as well as books. They also sponsor lectures on topics such as astrology, tarot cards, and past life regression. Books by the actress and New Age leader Shirley MacLaine are featured in these shops.

6

SETTING SAIL ON AN ASTRAL VOYAGE

CAROL ANN LIAROS once worked at the Human Dimensions Institute in Buffalo, New York. There she tried to teach blind people to "read" colors with their hands. She reports that a few seemed to make progress toward that goal. To her surprise, some of her subjects also learned to "mind travel" via OBEs. While fully relaxed, for instance, they pictured themselves flying to a friend's house. There they "saw" people and objects.

One woman described details as small as toys scattered on the front porch. A second subject said, "Awareness of my own energy field is developing . . . I feel as though I can really see myself. . . . I seem to be able to almost see what is in a room. It seems that I really see it, although I don't, and I am totally blind."[1]

Describing the technique of astral travel is simple. Whether the technique will work or not is a more complex question. Experts in the field say that almost all OBEs are pleasant. Most travelers want to go again and again. Only a handful of people say their OBEs turned into nightmares. These astral travelers tell of feeling pain, pressure, and terror.

Someone who seeks an OBE must be relaxed. One good way to calm the mind is to meditate. Find a quiet room and lie back against some pillows. With eyes closed, repeat a special sound over and over. Words like "ommmmm" with lots of m's seem to work well. Breathe deeply and clear the mind of all but that special word. Give the process ten or fifteen minutes. Do not be upset if distracting thoughts creep in. Resolve to try again the next day. After all, no one learns to play winning tennis the first day out. Learning to meditate takes practice, too.

Psychics believe that OBEs are related to the body's energy field—its aura. Kirlian photos show

Some people meditate by chanting while sitting in the lotus position. Experts say that simpler methods work, too. Staring into a candle flame helps screen out distracting thoughts.

A mandala is a geometric figure that always brings the eye back to the center. Because staring at a mandala screens out distracting thoughts, it can be used as an aid to meditation.

that all living things, plant and animal, produce distinctive auras. You may not have to depend on photos to see an aura, however. Take a friend (let's call her Nan) into a dimly lit room. Ask Nan to stand a foot away from a dark background. Face her from eight to ten feet away. Turn your head and look at her out of the corners of your eyes. With any luck, you will see her aura as a halo of light. [2]

Skeptics scoff at tests like this one. Auras, they say, are just clouds of water vapor. Colors appear, they explain, when light is refracted by the droplets. What skeptics cannot explain is the fact that auras appear to vary with the subject's health. Psychics claim they can diagnose illness by the shape and color of someone's aura.

Those who order themselves to see auras or go out-of-body are likely to fail. People who fear loss of contact seldom stray far from their bodies during an OBE. Others worry that they will meet evil spirits. It is said that most lose these fears as they glory in their new freedom. They often soar skyward, safe from earthly cares. The goal is to empty the mind and leave it open to the OBE. Some people reach that point fairly soon. Others take weeks or months to attain their first OBE.

Most of us do not reach that point, for reasons no one can explain. Even so, the effort is never wasted. Meditation does a good job of easing the stress of daily living . . . and that's a worthwhile goal all on its own.

Would you like to see an aura? First make a filter from a 7"x9" piece of dark blue cellophane taped into a cardboard frame. Stare at a light for a moment though the filter, then darken the room. Now look at a friend's hand through the filter. With luck, you will see flashes of light—the aura—around your friend's fingertips.

Notes by Chapter

Chapter 1

1. Stuart Holroyd, *Psychic Voyages* (Garden City, N.Y.: Doubleday, 1977), pp. 6--8.
2. Holroyd, pp. 86–88

Chapter 2

1. Brad Steiger, *Astral Projection* (Rockport, Mass.: Para Research, 1982), pp. 49–50.
2. The Bible, II Kings 6:8–22 (AV).
3. Rosemary Ellen Guiley, *Harper's Encyclopedia of Mystical & Paranormal Experience* (New York: HarperCollins, 1991), p. 420.
4. Herbert B. Greenhouse, *The Astral Journey* (Garden City, N.Y.: Doubleday, 1975), p. 23.
5. Charles A. Lindbergh, *Autobiography of Values* (NewYork: Harcourt Brace Jovanovich, 1976), pp. 11–12.

Chapter 3

1. Greenhouse, p. 189.
2. Holroyd, pp. 20–21.
3. Greenhouse, p. 188.
4. Benjamin Walker, *Beyond the Body* (London: Routledge & Kegan Paul, 1974), p. 65.
5. Greenhouse, pp. 46–47.
6. Greenhouse, pp. 187–188.
7. Guiley, p. 421.
8. Guiley, pp. 64–66.

Chapter 4

1. Holroyd, pp. 88–92.
2. Verlyn Klinkenborg, "At the Edge of Eternity," *Life* (March 1992), p. 66.
3. Carol Zaleski, *Otherworld Journeys: Accounts of*

Near-Death Experience in Medieval and Modern Times (New York: Oxford University Press, 1987), p. 122.

4. Hans Eysenck and Carl Sargent, *Explaining the Unexplained* (London: Weidenfield & Nicolson, 1982), p. 160.

5. Klinkenborg, p. 71.

6. Zaleski, p. 144.

Chapter 5

1. Guiley, pp. 422–423.

2. Editors of Time-Life, *Psychic Voyages* (Alexandria, Va.: Time-Life, 1987), pp. 35–36.

3. Time-Life, *Psychic Voyages*, p. 41.

4. Richard Broughton, *Parapsychology: The Controversial Science* (New York: Ballantine Books, 1991), pp. 249–251.

5. Time-Life, *Psychic Voyages*, p. 45.

Chapter 6

1. Greenhouse, pp. 339–340.

2. William Jon Watkins, *The Psychic Experiment Book* (Englewood Cliffs, N.J.: Prentice-Hall, 1980), pp. 44–45.

Glossary

apparition—An unexpected or unusual sight. Scientists generally prefer to use this term in place of the term "astral body."

astral body—Another name for the body double. During an OBE the astral body is said to leave the physical body as it begins its journeys.

astral travel—An older name for an OBE. Some psychics claim they can go astral traveling any time they wish.

aura—An ever-changing energy field that psychics say surrounds all living plants, animals, and people. Psychics claim they can diagnose illness by the shape and color of a person's aura.

body double—The nonphysical body that leaves the real body during an OBE. Body doubles are also called astral bodies or doppelgängers.

brain waves—Electric impulses produced by the brain, as measured on an EEG (electroencephalogram) machine. The three waves produced during waking hours are called alpha, beta, and theta. ESP powers appear to be strongest when the individual is in a relaxed alpha state.

clairvoyance—The power to perceive events that occur beyond the range of one's normal senses. Some researchers believe that what seem to be OBEs are really clairvoyant events.

hypnosis—A sleeplike state in which the subject will accept almost any suggestion made by the hypnotist.

Kirlian photos—Photographs taken of living organisms in the presence of a high-voltage electrical field. Kirlian photos show subjects surrounded by glowing, colored halos of light that are thought to be auras.

meditation—A process that relaxes the body by freeing the mind of all distracting thoughts.

near-death experience (NDE)—The feeling of having died and left one's body, only to return to life some time later.

New Age—A catch-all term for a broad collection of psychic beliefs. While few New Agers would agree on the details, most believe in OBEs, crystal power, ESP and past lives.

precognition—The power to foretell events before they happen.

prophet—A wise man or woman through whom the will of God (or the gods) is expressed.

psychic—Someone who claims powers that cannot be explained by natural law.

psychokinesis—The power to move or otherwise affect objects without touching them.

séance—A meeting at which people try to contact the spirits of the dead.

silver cord—The stretchy cord that is said to tie the body double to the physical body during an OBE.

skeptic—Someone who questions widely accepted beliefs or theories.

stowaway—Someone who hides on a ship or plane in order to obtain free passage.

telepathy—Mind-to-mind communication between two or more people.

More Good Reading About OBEs

Brennan, J. H. *The Astral Projection Workbook: How to Achieve Out-of-Body Experiences.* New York: Sterling Publishing, 1990.

Broughton, Richard S. *Parapsychology: The Controversial Science.* New York: Ballantine Books, 1991.

Editors of Time-Life Books. *Psychic Voyages.* Alexandria, Va.: Time-Life, 1987.

Eysenck, Hans and Carl Sargent. *Explaining the Unexplained.* London: Weidenfield & Nicolson, 1982.

Greenhouse, Herbert B. *The Astral Journey.* Garden City, N.Y.: Doubleday, 1975.

Holroyd, Stuart. *Psychic Voyages.* Garden City, N.Y.: Doubleday and Co., 1977.

Klinkenborg, Verlyn. "At the Edge of Eternity." *Life,* March 1992, pp. 65–73.

Moody, Raymond A. *Life After Life.* Harrisburg, Pa.: Stackpole Books, 1976.

Steiger, Brad. *Astral Projection.* Rockport, Mass.: Para Research, Inc., 1982.

Walker, Benjamin. *Beyond the Body: The Human Double and the Astral Planes.* London: Routledge & Kegan Paul, 1974.

Watkins, William Jon. *The Psychic Experiment Book.* Englewood Cliffs, N.J.: Prentice-Hall, 1980.

Zaleski, Carol. *Otherworld Journeys: Accounts of Near-Death Experience in Medieval and Modern Times.* New York: Oxford University Press, 1987.

Index